# WATCH OUT:

# *I'm Oily!*


**Natasha C. Johnson-Rouse**

**Watch Out: I'm Oily!**



HOV Publishing is a division of HOV, LLC.
email: hopeofvision@gmail.com
www.hovpub.com

Cover Design by Daphney Jules-Ogar
Interior layout design by HOV Design Solutions
Editor: HOV Publishing Editorial Team
Proofreading Editors: Felicia Patten and Shari Cameron

ISBN Paperback: 978-1-955107-09-9
ISBN eBook: 978-1-955107-08-2

Printed in the United States of America

# Dedication

To my dear Uncle Earnest,

The one who first whispered the power of the anointing into my heart.

You, with your unwavering belief in the divine call upon my life, showed me what it truly means to live soaked in God's presence. You taught me that the anointing is not just a gift but a mandate—to walk in obedience, to serve with joy, and to be a vessel of His holy purpose. Your steadfast encouragement echoed the words of 1 John 2:27: *"But the anointing which you have received from Him abides in you..."* You, my dear Uncle, embodied that anointing and became its living testimony, showing me that when we yield to the Holy Spirit, we are empowered to do all things through Christ, who strengthens us (Philippians 4:13).

I remember the countless hours you spent praying with me, sharing the mysteries of God's anointing, and urging me never to settle for less than His best. You introduced me to the holy oil that doesn't just cover but transforms, propels, and equips. You instilled in me the sacred truth that the anointing is not for our glory but for His—so that His work may be made known and His Kingdom advanced.

Uncle Earnest, you were my living example of what it looks like to walk in the fullness of God's anointing. The fire you ignited in me burns brightly today, and it will continue to burn as long as I draw breath. With every word written and every page turned, I am walking in the anointing you taught me to embrace.

Thank you for believing in me when I couldn't see it for myself. Thank you for sharing the anointing of God with me.

Continue to rest in peace and victory!

With love and eternal gratitude,

Your niece and buddy,

Natasha

# ACKNOWLEDGMENTS

Completing this book has truly been one of the most challenging yet fulfilling experiences of my life. Bringing it full circle tested my limits in ways I never anticipated, but the reward has been immeasurable. This journey would not have been possible without the incredible team by my side, whose support, guidance, and unwavering belief in this project helped me navigate every twist and turn.

To my Pastors—Rev. Dr. William D. Watley & Superintendent Larry C. Miles Sr.—whose guidance has been a profound blessing in my life, thank you for helping me recognize the calling and anointing in my life. Your wisdom, support, and unwavering faith have taught me how to fully embrace my purpose, walk confidently in my anointing, and love the God who has entrusted me with this gift. Your mentorship has shaped not only my spiritual journey but also the foundation upon which this book stands. I am forever grateful for your leadership and love.

To the prophetic voices in my life, thank you for refusing to let this prophecy fade. Your unwavering encouragement and belief in God's Word over my life have been a constant source of strength. You pushed me to step boldly into the season and purpose He ordained for me, reminding me to trust His timing and calling. Your words have been a guiding light, and I am forever grateful for your faithfulness in speaking life into this journey.

To my incredible Publishing Team, thank you for helping transform this dream into reality. Your collective expertise, dedication, and support have been invaluable throughout this journey. A special thank you to Mrs. Germaine Miller-Summers, my publisher, who guided me every step of the way with patience and understanding—your steady presence made all the difference. And to Daphney, thank you for being one of the most talented designers I know. Your creativity and ability to always understand the assignment brought the vision for the cover of my first book to life in ways I could have never imagined. I am deeply grateful for each of you and all you've contributed to this gift.

To my incredible, anointed sister friends—Pam, Tasha, Ayanna and Thurselle—thank you for your relentless encouragement and support. You believed in me when I had doubts, challenged me when I wanted to quit, and pushed me to reach beyond what I thought was possible. Your friendship has been a constant source of strength, and I am forever grateful for each of you.

To my editors, my sisters Felicia and Shari—both by blood and by heart—thank you for being the sharp eyes and loving hands that shaped this book into its final form. Your keen insights, thoughtful guidance, and tireless dedication have made all the difference. Beyond the work, your love and support have been a constant source of strength throughout this journey. I am deeply grateful to have you not only as my editors but as my beloved sisters.

To my entire immediate family, thank you for your endless love, support, and for giving me the time and space to complete this book. I thank you for your unwavering love, support, and patience throughout this journey. I am deeply grateful for the sacrifices you made, the moments we missed, and the understanding you extended as I dedicated time to completing this book. Because of all of you, this book is here, ready to be received as a gift to the world.

To my readers, may this book be exactly what you need to step forward—oily, empowered, and ready to live out the purpose God has uniquely designed for you. The time is **NOW.**

**Watch out, I'm oily!**

# WATCH OUT:
# I'm Oily!

# Contents

# WATCH OUT: *I'm Oily!*

# INTRODUCTION

I've often found myself reflecting on the incredible journey we each take through life—a journey that requires preparation, readiness, and fullness. It's not just about having the right knowledge or skills; it's about having the right heart, the right mindset, and being equipped to step into all that God has designed for us. It is with this deep conviction that I felt compelled to write this book.

Why? Because too many of us, especially women, have been conditioned to shrink back, to settle, or to wait for the "perfect moment." We've been told to put our dreams on hold, to wait until everything falls into place before we step forward. But I'm here to tell you—*the moment* is now. We cannot afford to wait. We are the vessels God has chosen for such a time as this, and it is time we show up fully, ready, and oiled for the assignment He has anointed us to carry out.

As a pastor, I've seen far too many people sit on the sidelines, unsure of their purpose, their power, or their potential. But let me remind you: *you are necessary*. God has called you for this moment, and He has equipped you with everything you need. The oil He has poured over you is not just for a season—it's for your life. And I want to help you recognize that, tap into it, and live a life of purpose, power, and passion.

This book is my gift to you. It's a guide, an encouragement, and a challenge to take a step toward being the woman God has called you to be. I want you to read this book with an open heart and a readiness to engage. Don't just read the words—*feel them*. Journal through the pages, reflect on what God is revealing to you. Take time to think about how you can be ready for what's next in your life. Grab your favorite cup of tea, call up a friend, and have a tea-time talk about being ready, being prepared, and being oiled for everything God wants to do in you and through you.

And don't worry if things get a little messy. Life isn't about perfection; it's about showing up, oil in hand, ready to be used for God's glory. Trust me, I've had my moments of feeling unprepared, but every time I leaned into God, He made a way. Now, it's your turn to embrace your calling and live out the fullness of what He has for you.

You're not here by accident. You were born for this time, for this moment. You are not a coincidence. You are necessary. And it is my prayer that as you read these pages, you will understand just how deeply God has prepared you for the life He has set before you.

So, let's dive in, let's get oily, and let's get ready. The world is waiting for the person you are becoming.

With love and excitement

# WATCH OUT:
# I'm Oily!

# CHAPTER
ONE
# THE OIL CRISIS

**Opening Illustration: Tires on the Road**

Let me take you on a journey. Picture yourself driving down a long stretch of highway. The sun is shining, the sky is clear, and your destination is in sight. But as you press down on the accelerator, something feels off. The car isn't responding the way it should. It's sluggish, and you realize that the tires are under-inflated. You pull over and check the tires, and sure enough, they're low on air. Without enough air, the tires can't perform at their best. The car struggles, and your journey becomes harder, slower, and more dangerous.

Now, imagine your spiritual life as that car, and the oil of God as the air in those tires. Just like a car needs the right amount of air to move smoothly and safely down the road, we need the oil of God to navigate the journey of life. Without it, we become sluggish, our progress is hindered, and we risk running into danger. This is the oil crisis we face today—not just on the road, but in our souls.

## The Concept of an Oil Crisis

We've all heard about oil crises in the world—those moments when the price of oil skyrockets, or when nations go to war over this precious resource. It's a crisis that disrupts economies, shakes governments, and impacts every aspect of our daily lives. But there's another oil crisis that's far more dangerous, and it's one that's not making the headlines. It's the spiritual oil crisis that's gripping our churches, our homes, and our workplaces.

What do I mean by a spiritual oil crisis? It's the lack of God's anointing, the absence of His presence and power in our lives. We are living in a time where many have forgotten the necessity of having the oil of God. Some don't know they need it, and others think they can live without it. But let me tell you, beloved, the oil of God is not optional—it is essential.

## The Necessity of God's Oil

The oil of God is what keeps us going when the road gets rough. It's what destroys the yoke of bondage, what lights our path in the darkest valleys, and what enables us to shine brightly in a world full of darkness. Without the oil of God, we are like those under-inflated tires—struggling to move forward, at risk of a blowout, and unable to reach our destination.

Money can buy you comfort, relationships can bring you joy, but only the oil of God can sustain you in the assignments He's given you. It's the oil that gives you the strength to walk in integrity, to live out your calling, and to withstand the pressures of life. It's the oil that allows you to be a light in a dark world, to bring hope to the hopeless, and to stand firm in the face of adversity.

**The Spiritual Oil Crisis in Our Lives**

Now, let's get real. Many of us are dealing with an oil crisis in our own lives. Maybe you're feeling spiritually dry, disconnected from God, or overwhelmed by the challenges you're facing. Maybe you've been running on empty for so long that you've forgotten what it feels like to be full of God's presence. If that's you, it's time to recognize the crisis and do something about it.

We can't afford to ignore the signs of an oil crisis. Just like a car with under-inflated tires, we risk damaging ourselves and those around us if we try to keep going without addressing the issue. We need to pull over, check our spiritual gauges, and get filled up with the oil of God.

**Interactive Element: Reflecting on Your Spiritual Oil Crisis**

Let's take a moment to reflect. Think about the areas in your life where you're feeling the strain, where you're struggling to move forward, or where you've lost your sense of purpose and direction. These are the areas where you might be experiencing a spiritual oil crisis.

___

___

___

___

___

___

___

___

___

___

___

___

___

___

___

**Take a few minutes to write down your thoughts:**

- Where in your life do you feel spiritually dry or disconnected from God?

  ______________________________________________

  ______________________________________________

  ______________________________________________

- Are there areas where you're struggling to maintain your faith, your hope, or your joy?

  ______________________________________________

  ______________________________________________

  ______________________________________________

- What challenges are you facing that seem overwhelming or impossible to overcome?

  ______________________________________________

  ______________________________________________

  ______________________________________________

- Do you feel like you're running on empty, trying to keep up with the demands of life without the strength or energy to do so?

  ______________________________________________

  ______________________________________________

  ______________________________________________

As you write, ask God to reveal the areas where you need His oil the most. Invite Him to fill you with His presence, to refresh and renew your spirit, and to give you the strength and power you need to keep moving forward.

Remember, recognizing the crisis is the first step to overcoming it. Once you've identified the areas where you need God's oil, commit to seeking Him daily, asking for His anointing, and allowing Him to fill you up so that you can continue the journey with strength and purpose.

Let this be the moment where you turn back to the source of your strength, where you refill your spiritual tank, and where you reclaim the oil of God that you need to fulfill the calling on your life. The oil crisis ends here, because God is ready and willing to pour out His oil on those who seek Him. All you have to do is ask.

_______________________________________________

_______________________________________________

_______________________________________________

_______________________________________________

_______________________________________________

_______________________________________________

_______________________________________________

# CHAPTER
TWO

## THE PARABLE of the 10 VIRGINS

### Understanding the Parable

As we zoom into our text for this evening, we find ourselves face to face with one of the most profound teachings of Jesus—the Parable of the 10 Virgins. The Book of Matthew contains several of Jesus' parables, and some of them are found exclusively in this Gospel, including this parable. Jesus shared this teaching just before He went to Jerusalem to be crucified. His disciples were eager to know more about the signs of His coming into power and the end of the age. There were aspects of His coming that they did not fully understand yet, but Jesus took the time to explain these signs and to teach them how they should live as they awaited His return.

This parable, like all of Jesus' teachings, is rich with meaning. It's a story about readiness, preparation, and the importance of being spiritually awake. But it's also a story that challenges us to examine our own lives and ask ourselves if we are truly prepared for what God has in store for us.

## Signs of the End of the Age

Before we dive into the parable itself, let's consider the context. The disciples were curious—like many of us are today—about the end times. They wanted to know the signs, the markers that would indicate when Jesus would come into His full power and when the end of the age would be upon them. They were seeking clarity, something that we all can relate to. How often do we find ourselves in situations where we desperately need understanding, where we long for a roadmap to guide us through the unknown?

Let me pause right here, people of God, and share an important truth: we do not have all the answers. And that's okay. We need wisdom, and we need knowledge to do what God has called us to do. Instead of walking around life confused and unfulfilled, we must take time to ask our Creator. The One who designed us has the answers we seek. He knows the questions we need to ask and the steps we need to take.

## Seeking Clarity from God

It's easy to get caught up in the hustle and bustle of life, to move forward without really understanding where we're going or why we're doing what we're doing. But God never intended for us to live in confusion or to stumble through life aimlessly. He has a plan for each of us—a plan that is meant to bring us into a bright future, not to harm us, but to prosper us and bring us to an expected end.

But here's the catch: we need to be in tune with God's plan. We need clarity. And that clarity doesn't come from the world, it doesn't come from the latest self-help book or the most popular podcast. It comes from God alone. The disciples needed clarity on certain aspects—they were not clear on everything He was saying, not clear on everything He was talking about. So what did they do? They asked the right One. They went to Jesus, the source of all wisdom and understanding.

**The Importance of Asking God**

In our own lives, how often do we seek clarity from the wrong sources? How many times do we rely on our own understanding, or worse, the opinions of others, rather than going directly to God? The disciples set an example for us—they asked Jesus to explain what they didn't understand. They sought wisdom from the One who holds all the answers.

We need to follow their example. When we're uncertain, when we're confused, when we're feeling lost, we need to pause and ask God for clarity. Don't make a move without Him. Get clarity so we are not following Christ amiss, so we are not following in error, so we are not living hollow and deceptive lives. There is a plan that God has for our lives—plans to bring us into a bright future, not plans to harm us, but plans that are good for us, that bring us to an expected end.

**The Parable: A Story of Readiness**

Now, let's dive into the parable itself. Jesus tells the story of ten virgins who took their lamps and went out to meet the bridegroom. Five of them were wise, and five were foolish. The wise virgins took oil in jars along with their lamps, but the foolish ones took their lamps but did not take any oil with them.

As the bridegroom was a long time in coming, they all became drowsy and fell asleep. But at midnight, the cry rang out: 'Here's the bridegroom! Come out to meet him!' Then all the virgins woke up and trimmed their lamps. The foolish ones said to the wise, 'Give us some of your oil; our lamps are going out.'

But the wise virgins replied, 'No, there may not be enough for both us and you. Instead, go to those who sell oil and buy some for yourselves.'

But while they were on their way to buy the oil, the bridegroom arrived. The virgins who were ready went in with him to the wedding banquet. And the door was shut. Later the others also came. 'Lord, Lord,' they said, 'open the door for us!' But he replied, 'Truly I tell you, I don't know you.'

Therefore, keep watch, because you do not know the day or the hour.

**The Lessons of the Parable**

This parable is rich with lessons for us. It teaches us about the importance of being prepared, of keeping watch, and of making sure that we have what we need to sustain us for the journey. It's a reminder that we cannot borrow someone else's oil—we cannot rely on the faith or the preparation of others. We must be responsible for our own spiritual readiness.

The oil in this parable represents the Holy Spirit, the presence of God in our lives. It's the anointing that we need to be effective in our walk with Christ. Without it, our lamps will go out—we will lose our way, and we will miss out on the promises that God has for us.

## Applying the Parable to Our Lives

So how do we apply this parable to our lives? First, we must recognize the importance of being spiritually prepared. We cannot afford to be like the foolish virgins who waited until the last minute to try to get what they needed. We must be diligent in our pursuit of God, in our prayer life, in our study of the Word, and in our obedience to His leading.

Second, we need to keep watch. Jesus is coming back, and we don't know the day or the hour. But it's not just about His return—it's about being ready for whatever God has for us, whether it's a new opportunity, a challenge, or a blessing. We need to be spiritually awake, alert, and ready to respond when God calls.

Finally, we need to seek clarity from God in all things. Just as the disciples asked Jesus to explain the signs of the end of the age, we must go to God with our questions, our doubts, and our confusion. He is the source of all wisdom, and He will guide us into all truth.

## Interactive Element: Seeking Clarity and Readiness

Let's take a moment to reflect. Think about your own life—are there areas where you need clarity from God? Are there situations where you've been trying to figure things out on your own, instead of going to God for answers?

**Take a few minutes to write down your thoughts:**

- What are the areas in your life where you feel uncertain or confused?

  ______________________________

  ______________________________

  ______________________________

  ______________________________

  ______________________________

- Have you been seeking clarity from God, or have you been relying on your own understanding?

  ______________________________

  ______________________________

  ______________________________

  ______________________________

  ______________________________

- Are you spiritually prepared for what God has in store for you? Do you have the oil you need to keep your lamp burning?

  ______________________________

  ______________________________

  ______________________________

  ______________________________

As you write, ask God to reveal the areas where you need more of His oil, more of His presence in your life. Commit to seeking Him daily, to keeping watch, and to being ready for whatever He has in store for you.

Remember, the parable of the 10 virgins is not just a story—it's a call to action. It's a reminder that we must be diligent in our walk with God, that we must seek Him with all our hearts, and that we must be ready for His return. Let this chapter be a turning point in your life, a moment where you choose to live with intention, with purpose, and with the clarity that comes from seeking God above all else.

# WATCH OUT:
# I'm Oily!

# CHAPTER
THREE

# THE COST of PURITY

**Understanding the Cost of Purity**

In a world that values popularity, quick results, and instant gratification, it's easy to lose sight of the value of purity. But let me tell you, being set apart, being pure, and waiting on God's timing is not just a choice—it's a costly commitment. It's a lifestyle that may require sacrifice, discipline, and patience, but in the end, the rewards are worth every moment.

We live in a world where people often seek validation, approval, and direction from sources outside of God's will. We ask the wrong people about what we need to wait for. We seek advice from people who don't know God, who don't understand His timing, and who may not even believe in His promises. But if we want to live a life that is set apart, a life that is pure, we need to align ourselves with people who are walking the same path, who share the same values, and who are willing to wait on God's timing.

## The Importance of Surrounding Yourself with the Right People

Let's talk about your circle—those people who are closest to you, who influence you, and who speak into your life. You see, the people you surround yourself with matter. If you're serious about pursuing God's will, about maintaining your purity, and about waiting on His timing, you need to be around like-minded people. Staying around the minds of people who are content with the status quo, who don't value purity, and who aren't willing to wait, will only pull you further away from your purpose.

You need to get around the people who are doing what you need to be doing to wait. Those are those who embody humility, grace, love, peace, wisdom, joy—those who won't take but are ready to give. When you surround yourself with people like this, you are surrounding yourself with strength. These are the people who will lift you up when you feel weak, who will pray with you when you need encouragement, and who will remind you of God's promises when you feel like giving up.

There's a saying that you become like the five people you spend the most time with. So, ask yourself: are you surrounding yourself with people who are helping you move closer to God's plan, or are they distracting you from it?

**Finding Your Circle of Strength**

In this journey, it's crucial to have a circle of individuals who understand the cost of purity, who know what it means to wait on God's timing, and who are committed to walking this path alongside you. These people are not selfish; they are ready to assist, to guide, and to support you as you wait patiently on the Lord's plan for your life.

**Repeat after me**

My circle is waiting for me! They have what I need to help me. They are not just friends; they are my brothers & sisters in Christ, my prayer warriors, my accountability partners.

Let's be clear: finding this kind of circle may require you to make some difficult choices. It may mean letting go of relationships that no longer serve God's purpose in your life. It may mean distancing yourself from people who discourage you, who speak negativity over your dreams, or who tempt you to compromise your purity. But remember, purity comes at a cost, and that cost may include pruning relationships that are not aligned with God's purpose for you.

**The Example of the 10 Virgins**

Jesus wanted His disciples to be ready, spiritually prepared for the coming wait, but excited for the promise of His return. He told them the Parable of the 10 Virgins to illustrate what the ready will look like, as well as what the unready will look like. Five of the virgins were wise—they were prepared, they had their oil, and they were ready for the bridegroom's arrival. The other five were foolish—they were unprepared, they lacked oil which caused them to have missed out on the blessing.

What made the difference between the wise and the foolish virgins? It was their readiness, their willingness to be prepared, and their understanding of the cost. The wise virgins knew that purity, readiness, and patience would require sacrifice, but they were willing to pay the price. They understood that the blessing of being in the presence of the bridegroom was worth more than anything else.

## Purity is Not Passive—It's a Daily Commitment

Purity is not a one-time decision; it's a daily commitment. It's choosing to walk in integrity, to guard your heart, and to live a life that is pleasing to God. Purity is about more than abstaining from certain behaviors; it's about cultivating a heart that is set apart, that seeks God above all else, and that is willing to wait on His timing.

Let's be honest—this kind of purity is not easy. It may mean turning down invitations, saying no to certain relationships, or choosing a path that is less popular. It may mean spending more time in prayer, seeking God's guidance, and resisting the temptation to take shortcuts. But remember, the cost of purity is nothing compared to the blessings that come from being in alignment with God's will.

## The Reward of Purity

When you choose to live a life of purity, you are choosing to live a life that is set apart, that is filled with purpose, and that is blessed by God. You are choosing to be a light in a dark world, to be an example of God's love, and to be a vessel of His grace. The reward of purity is a life that is filled with peace, joy, and the assurance that you are walking in God's will.

Remember, the five wise virgins were not only prepared, but they were also filled with joy and anticipation for the bridegroom's arrival. They were excited because they knew that their preparation would lead to a beautiful encounter with the bridegroom. In the same way, when we commit to a life of purity, we can look forward to the blessings that God has in store for us.

**Embracing the Cost of Purity**

Choosing purity is not about being perfect; it's about being purposeful. It's about making a conscious decision every day to walk in integrity, to guard your heart, and to seek God's will above all else. Yes, it will cost you something. It may cost you friendships, opportunities, or moments of temporary pleasure. But in the end, the cost of purity is nothing compared to the eternal rewards that come from living a life that is fully surrendered to God.

So, embrace the cost of purity. Surround yourself with people who encourage you, who lift you up, and who remind you of God's promises. Seek clarity from God, and trust Him to guide you every step of the way. And remember, you are not alone. God is with you, and He will provide everything you need to walk this path of purity with strength, grace, and joy.

## Interactive Element: Reflecting on the Cost of Purity

Now, let's take a moment to reflect on the cost of purity in your own life. Think about the areas where you may need to make sacrifices, where you may need to distance yourself from certain relationships, or where you may need to strengthen your commitment to purity.

**Take a few minutes to journal your thoughts:**

- Are there relationships in your life that are pulling you away from God's purpose?

  ____________________________________________
  ____________________________________________
  ____________________________________________
  ____________________________________________

- Are you surrounding yourself with people who encourage you in your walk with God, or do you need to seek out a new circle?

  ____________________________________________
  ____________________________________________
  ____________________________________________
  ____________________________________________

- What sacrifices are you willing to make to maintain your purity and to live a life that is set apart for God?

  ____________________________________________
  ____________________________________________
  ____________________________________________
  ____________________________________________
  ____________________________________________

- What areas of your life do you need to surrender to God, trusting Him to provide clarity, strength, and support?

  ________________________________________

  ________________________________________

  ________________________________________

  ________________________________________

As you reflect and journal your thoughts, ask God to reveal any areas where you may be compromising your purity, where you may need to make adjustments, and where you may need His guidance.

Pray for the strength to let go of anything that is hindering your walk with Him, and for the courage to pursue a life of purity, no matter the cost.

____________________________________________

____________________________________________

____________________________________________

____________________________________________

____________________________________________

____________________________________________

____________________________________________

____________________________________________

# WATCH OUT:
# *I'm Oily!*

# CHAPTER
FOUR

## BRING Your LAMP

### The Call to Readiness

In the parable of the 10 Virgins, Jesus brings us into the lives of ten women waiting expectantly for the arrival of the bridegroom. This parable isn't just a story about waiting—it's a profound lesson on preparation, expectation, and the importance of having what we need to fulfill the call of God. These ten women are all set apart, pure, waiting for something significant. But the difference between those who were wise and those who were foolish was in what they brought with them.

Jesus was showing us that there's a distinction in waiting for what you're expecting versus waiting without expectation. When you expect something, you're prepared, you're looking for it. But if you're not expecting anything, you're distracted, you're unfocused, and you're unprepared.

I enjoy waiting for my Amazon packages to arrive. I track it, I know the delivery time, and I am constantly checking my Alexa for notification to see if the package has arrived or if I had any new updates. Every sound on Alexa gets my attention because I'm expecting the arrival of something great; something new. Now, if I wasn't expecting the package, I'd probably forget about it or not even notice when it arrived! When we don't expect something, I am unfocused and not prepared for its arrival. Yet, when I am expecting something, I make sure that I am prepared, attentive, and ready for it. The same goes for life—when you expect something good, you'll be prepared to recognize it and act on it when it comes your way.

So what are you waiting for? Are you waiting with expectancy for what God has in store, or are you passively going through life, unsure of what you need and unprepared for what's coming?

**Bring What You Have**

"Bring what you have." These four words carry so much weight. In this parable, all ten women are virgins. This is significant because it symbolizes purity, a life set apart, a heart that is willing to wait on God's timing. To be a virgin means more than abstaining from certain behaviors; it's a choice to live a life that is undefiled, dedicated, and set apart for something holy.

In Revelation 14:4-5, the followers of Jesus are described as virgins who "follow the Lamb wherever He goes" and who are "blameless." This purity is not just about physical abstinence; it's about spiritual integrity and a lifestyle that reflects a commitment to God. These ten women were not just physically pure; they were spiritually set apart. They were not part of the popular crowd, they weren't following the trends, and they weren't traveling the wide road. They had chosen the narrow path, the path less traveled, the path that requires commitment, sacrifice, and the willingness to bring what you have.

**Being Set Apart**

To be set apart is to live a life that looks different from the world around you. It's choosing God's way even when it's not the easiest path. God's way may not be the easiest, but it's always the best. It's a journey that shapes your character, strengthens your faith, and leads to true fulfillment. The easy way might promise comfort, but it's the hard way that brings lasting transformation. Trusting God's path means choosing purpose over ease—and that's where true growth happens.

These ten virgins had made a choice to live differently, to avoid the common and to pursue the sacred. They were not part of a "mixed breed," meaning they hadn't compromised their values, they hadn't allowed the world's influence to dilute their commitment to God. They were chosen, and they lived like it.

Being set apart is not about isolation; it's about purpose. God doesn't call us to be set apart so we can stand alone, but so we can be prepared to serve Him fully. When we set ourselves apart, we're making room for God's presence in our lives, we're making space for His anointing, and we're positioning ourselves to be used by Him.

**The Lamp and the Oil: Symbols of Readiness**

In the parable, all ten women brought lamps with them. But here's the catch—five of them brought extra oil, while the other five did not. The lamp symbolizes our lives, our outward witness, and the light we carry as followers of Christ. The oil, however, represents the inward anointing, the Holy Spirit's presence in our lives, the strength that sustains us when our own strength runs out.

The five wise virgins understood that bringing their lamps wasn't enough—they needed oil to keep the lamps burning. They knew the wait might be long, that the journey might be difficult, and that they would need more than just an initial spark. They brought extra oil because they were ready for the long haul; they were prepared to endure until the bridegroom arrived.

The foolish virgins, on the other hand, had their lamps, but they didn't have enough oil. They didn't prepare for the journey ahead. They showed up looking like they were ready, but their readiness was only surface-deep. When the bridegroom arrived, their lamps were going out, and they had nothing left to sustain them.

### What Does It Mean to "Bring Your Lamp"?

Bringing your lamp means bringing your life, your testimony, your gifts, and your faith. It means showing up with everything you have, ready to serve, ready to wait, and ready to shine. But bringing your lamp without bringing extra oil is like starting a journey without packing any supplies. It's a surface-level commitment that won't last when things get tough.

In this journey of faith, bringing your lamp isn't enough. You need the oil of God to keep that lamp burning. The oil represents your prayer life, your relationship with God, your dedication to seeking Him daily. It's the fuel that keeps you going when the night is long and the wait seems endless. Without the oil, your lamp will go out, and you'll be left in darkness.

## Bringing Extra Oil: Preparing for the Unexpected

The wise virgins brought extra oil because they were prepared for the unexpected. They didn't know when the bridegroom would come, but they were ready for however long it would take. They anticipated the wait, they prepared for the delays, and they made sure they had enough to sustain them.

Life is full of unexpected moments—times when we're required to go the extra mile, to endure a little longer, to wait a little more. Bringing extra oil means being spiritually prepared for whatever comes our way. It means filling ourselves up with God's presence so that we're not running on empty when challenges arise.

Are you bringing extra oil, or are you just bringing your lamp? Are you prepared to endure, or are you just hoping things will work out? Bringing extra oil requires intentionality. It requires spending time with God, building up your spiritual reserves, and being ready for whatever He has in store.

## Living with Expectation and Readiness

In the end, the parable of the 10 Virgins is a call to live with expectation. It's a reminder that we're not just waiting for something insignificant—we're waiting for the bridegroom, for the fulfillment of God's promises, for the return of Christ. And in that waiting, we're called to bring what we have, to bring our lamps, our lives, our testimonies, and to make sure we're filled with the oil of God.

This is not a passive waiting; it's an active, intentional, prepared waiting. It's living with the expectation that God has something incredible in store and being ready to step into it when the time comes. So bring your lamp, bring your oil, and bring your heart fully surrendered to God. The wait may be long, but with the oil of God, you'll have everything you need to endure, to shine, and to be ready when He calls.

As you move forward, remember that the journey requires both the lamp and the oil. It requires your life and God's anointing, your commitment and His presence. Don't be caught unprepared. Live with expectation, bring what you have, and trust that God will provide the strength, the oil, and the guidance you need to reach the destination He has for you.

**Interactive Element: Reflecting on Your Lamp and Your Oil**

Let's take a moment to reflect on your own life. Think about the areas where you may be relying on your own strength, where you may be showing up with a lamp but without enough oil.

**Take a few minutes to journal your thoughts:**

- Are you bringing your lamp and your oil, or are you relying on surface-level commitment?

  ______________________________________________

  ______________________________________________

  ______________________________________________

  ______________________________________________

- Are there areas in your life where you're running low on oil, where you need a fresh filling of God's Spirit?

  ______________________________________________

  ______________________________________________

  ______________________________________________

  ______________________________________________

- What does "bringing extra oil" look like in your life? Is it spending more time in prayer, diving deeper into the Word, or surrounding yourself with people who encourage your faith?

  ______________________________________________

  ______________________________________________

  ______________________________________________

  ______________________________________________

  ______________________________________________

As you write, ask God to reveal the areas where you need more oil, more of His presence, and more of His anointing. Commit to seeking Him daily, to filling yourself up with His Spirit, and to being ready for whatever He has in store.

# WATCH OUT:

# I'm Oily!

# CHAPTER
## FIVE

# THE CRISIS of UNPREPAREDNESS

### Understanding the Cost of Preparation

Let's take a moment, to pause right here and recognize a hard truth: having the oil of God in your life is going to cost you something. This isn't a "cheap grace" that we're talking about; this isn't something you can pick up casually and expect to keep without some level of sacrifice. The women in the parable who had the oil were prepared. They had paid the price for their readiness. And, beloved, to be spiritually prepared, to carry the oil of God's anointing, will require you to make sacrifices. You may have to let go of friends who don't support your walk with God, you may have to end relationships that pull you away from His purpose, and you may have to lay down your own agenda to pick up His.

This is a crisis of unpreparedness. So many believers want the oil, want the blessing, want the favor of God, but they are not willing to pay the cost of being prepared. They show up with their lamps, they look the part, but when the moment of testing comes, they have nothing to sustain them. They haven't invested in the oil, they haven't put in the time, and they haven't made the sacrifices necessary to carry the presence of God with them.

**The Purity of the Oil-Carriers**

The parable describes these women as virgins, which signifies more than just physical purity—it represents spiritual integrity and a life that is set apart. They weren't entangled in the distractions of the world; they were fully dedicated to their purpose, to waiting on the bridegroom. They had "nothing attached to them," as the saying goes. They were pure in heart, pure in mind, and pure in intention.

And this purity, this dedication, this readiness came at a cost. They didn't allow themselves to be swayed by popular opinion, by the trends of the world, or by the expectations of others. They were willing to stand apart, to be different, to be holy because they knew the value of what they carried. They knew the oil was worth more than any temporary pleasure, any fleeting popularity, or any passing relationship.

## Being Set Apart: The Importance of Purity in Readiness

Let me speak directly to you, people of God: when you are a virgin in God, when you are committed to carrying the oil of His anointing, you have to be okay with being set apart. You have to be okay with not fitting in, with not following the crowd, and with not being understood by everyone around you. Because if you're not willing to stand apart, if you're not willing to protect what God has given you, then you risk losing the purity of your calling.

To be set apart means guarding what God has placed within you. It means staying focused on your assignment, even when others are pulling you in different directions. It means saying "no" to what's popular and saying "yes" to what's pure. If you're constantly chasing after the approval of others, constantly trying to fit in, you'll end up compromising the purity of your oil. And, beloved, your oil is too valuable to let it be diluted by the world.

This is why, when you're new to carrying the oil of God, when you're new to this assignment thing, when you're new to walking in God's will, you can't afford to run in packs. You can't afford to run with what's popular or who is popular because, ultimately, your calling requires purity. You have to keep yourself in a place of integrity, with pure intentions, a pure heart, and a right spirit.

When you're set apart, the pastor won't have to worry about your motives because your life speaks for itself. High five your neighbor and say, "Be okay with being a virgin." Be okay with being set apart.

### The Crisis of Unpreparedness in Today's World

In today's world, there is a crisis of unpreparedness among believers. We see people who are willing to show up to church, willing to sing the songs, willing to carry the lamp, but not willing to make the sacrifices required to carry the oil. They want the appearance of readiness without the preparation that comes with it. They want the benefits of the anointing without the discipline that sustains it.

It's a tragic thing to be on assignment from God, to be called for a purpose, and yet be unprepared to fulfill it. It's heartbreaking to see someone with potential, with talent, and with a calling, but lacking the oil to carry them through. And this unpreparedness doesn't just impact the individual—it affects everyone around them. When we fail to be prepared, when we neglect to bring the oil, we miss out on the fullness of what God has for us, and we leave others without the light we were called to bring.

## Guarding Your Oil: Protecting What God Has Given You

Beloved, it's time to get serious about guarding the oil that God has given you. You may have to make some difficult decisions. You may have to set boundaries with people who don't respect your commitment to purity. You may have to walk away from situations that threaten to compromise your integrity. But remember, your oil is worth it. Your calling is worth it. Your purpose is worth it.

Protecting your oil means saying "no" to anything that tries to distract you from God's purpose. It means setting your mind on things above, not on the temporary pleasures and pressures of this world. It means being intentional about your relationships, surrounding yourself with people who uplift you, who support your journey, and who encourage your growth in Christ.

## Embracing the Cost of Preparation

Living a life that is set apart, a life that is filled with the oil of God's anointing, is not an easy journey. It requires sacrifice, it demands discipline, and it challenges us to live differently. But in the end, the cost of preparation is worth it. Because when the bridegroom arrives, when the moment of testing comes, those who are prepared, those who have paid the price, will be ready to step into the fullness of God's purpose.

So embrace the cost of preparation. Guard your oil, protect what God has given you, and be willing to stand apart for the sake of your calling. Remember, you are not alone. God is with you, and He will provide everything you need to walk this path of readiness with strength, grace, and purity.

Choose today to live a life that is prepared, that is filled with the oil of God, and that is set apart for His glory. The journey may be challenging, but the destination is worth it. Let this be the moment where you commit to living with intention, with purpose, and with the readiness that comes from being fully surrendered to God. The crisis of unpreparedness ends here. Step into the fullness of your calling, and let your life shine with the light of His anointing.

## Embracing the Cost of Preparation

Living a life that is set apart, a life that is filled with the oil of God's anointing, is not an easy journey. It requires sacrifice, it demands discipline, and it challenges us to live differently. But in the end, the cost of preparation is worth it. Because when the bridegroom arrives, when the moment of testing comes, those who are prepared, those who have paid the price, will be ready to step into the fullness of God's purpose.

So embrace the cost of preparation. Guard your oil, protect what God has given you, and be willing to stand apart for the sake of your calling. Remember, you are not alone. God is with you, and He will provide everything you need to walk this path of readiness with strength, grace, and purity.

Choose today to live a life that is prepared, that is filled with the oil of God, and that is set apart for His glory. The journey may be challenging, but the destination is worth it. Let this be the moment where you commit to living with intention, with purpose, and with the readiness that comes from being fully surrendered to God. The crisis of unpreparedness ends here. Step into the fullness of your calling, and let your life shine with the light of His anointing.

**Interactive Element: Reflecting on the Cost of Preparation**

Let's take a moment to reflect on the cost of preparation in your own life. Think about the areas where you may need to make sacrifices, where you may need to guard your oil, and where you may need to strengthen your commitment to purity.

**Take a few minutes to journal your thoughts:**

- Are there relationships or habits in your life that are diluting your oil?

  ______________________________________________

  ______________________________________________

  ______________________________________________

  ______________________________________________

- What sacrifices are you willing to make to protect your oil and to live a life that is set apart for God?

  ______________________________________________

  ______________________________________________

  ______________________________________________

  ______________________________________________

  ______________________________________________

- What areas of your life do you need to surrender to God, trusting Him to give you the strength and discipline to stay prepared?

  ______________________________________________

  ______________________________________________

  ______________________________________________

  ______________________________________________

  ______________________________________________

As you reflect, ask God to reveal any areas where you may be compromising your readiness, where you may need to make adjustments, and where you may need His guidance. Pray for the strength to let go of anything that is hindering your walk with Him, and for the courage to pursue a life of purity and readiness, no matter the cost.

# WATCH OUT:

# *I'm Oily!*

# CHAPTER
## SIX

## THE POWER of OBEDIENCE

### Understanding Obedience and Assignment

In the Parable of the Ten Virgins, Jesus teaches us about the importance of readiness, but beneath that message lies a deeper truth about obedience. The ten virgins knew they had an assignment. They understood that their role was to meet the bridegroom and light the way to the celebration. Yet, only five were truly prepared to carry out this assignment because they were obedient to what was necessary - bringing both their lamps and the oil to sustain them.

As we walk the Christian journey, two key concepts often come to the forefront: obedience and assignment. While these terms are sometimes used interchangeably, they carry distinct significance, especially when we view them through the lens of Scripture. One of the most powerful parables that can help us understand these concepts is the Parable of the Ten Virgins (Matthew 25:1-13). This parable offers a clear view of the critical importance of obedience in the fulfillment of divine assignments.

Obedience is the act of following a command, instruction, or directive given by God. It is a choice to submit to the will of God, regardless of the circumstances, because we trust His plan. Obedience is not merely an outward action; it flows from a heart that desires to honor God and align with His purpose. Obedience is more than just following rules; it's an act of faith, trust, and reverence for God.

Assignment, on the other hand, refers to the specific task or purpose God gives to each believer. Every Christian has a unique assignment—something they are called to do to advance God's Kingdom on Earth. An assignment is a divine calling, a responsibility given by God to carry out specific work. It can be seasonal, but it is always connected to God's eternal purposes.

While obedience is the foundation for walking out our assignment, it is crucial to understand that our assignment will not be fulfilled without an obedient heart. The ten virgins provide a perfect example of how obedience and assignment go hand in hand.

The ten virgins were given the same assignment: to wait for the bridegroom. Their assignment was clear, but the execution of it revealed their differing levels of obedience. The wise virgins were obedient to the preparation process. They understood that to fulfill their assignment, they needed to be ready, not just outwardly but inwardly as well. They were obedient to bring extra oil, ensuring they would be prepared for the long wait.

**Obedience and the Anointing**

It is the anointing of the Holy Spirit that empowers us to obey. Obedience is not something we can accomplish on our own strength. The anointing is God's divine enablement, and it plays a critical role in both understanding and executing our assignment.

In 1 John 2:20, we read, “But you have an anointing from the Holy One, and you know all things.” The anointing gives us wisdom, insight, and the power to obey. It opens our eyes to the deeper meaning behind God’s commands and empowers us to carry out His will, no matter how challenging it may be.

Without the anointing, obedience becomes a mere act of willpower, and our assignments will often remain unfulfilled. The Holy Spirit equips us with the strength to persevere, even when it seems like the bridegroom is delayed. It is through the anointing that we are given the endurance to wait, the discernment to recognize the times, and the wisdom to stay prepared.

**Bring Your Lamp: Preparing for the Assignment**

The parable emphasizes that the ten virgins brought lamps with them, but there's a profound truth in this simple act. The lamp represents their responsibility, their faith, and their calling. Bringing the lamp was an act of obedience—it was their way of saying, "I'm ready to fulfill my part in this assignment."

Likewise, each of us is called to bring our lamps to the table. Your lamp might represent your talents, your time, your faith, or your resources. Whatever it is, God is asking you to bring it, to offer it up, and to be ready to use it for His glory. But bringing the lamp is only the first step. Without oil, the lamp cannot shine. Without obedience to seek God's presence and provision, the lamp remains just an empty vessel.

Obedience to God often requires preparation. It's not enough to hear the call; we must act in obedience. In this parable, the foolish virgins represent those who may hear the call but fail to prepare. They were disobedient in not bringing enough oil, failing to recognize that their assignment required diligence, foresight, and readiness.

## The Role of the Lamp and Oil in Jewish Tradition

In Jewish marital customs, the bridegroom's arrival was a moment of great celebration, often accompanied by ceremony and formalities. The bridesmaids' lamps were more than decorative—they served a critical purpose in lighting the bridegroom's way into the bride's home. This act was symbolic of honor, preparation, and joy for the union about to take place.

The ten virgins knew their assignment. They knew that their lamps were essential for the bridegroom's arrival and for initiating the celebration. Without the lamps, there would be no light to guide the way, no welcome for the bridegroom, and no fulfillment of their role in the ceremony.

## The Connection Between Obedience and Readiness

Jesus uses this parable to teach us about the coming of the kingdom of God, but there is also a clear message about obedience and readiness for the assignments God gives us. The five wise virgins were not just ready for the bridegroom—they were obedient to the call of preparation. They anticipated the need for extra oil, they took the time to gather what was necessary, and they remained vigilant, even as the night grew long.

Obedience, in this context, means taking the steps to prepare for what God has called you to do, even when it's inconvenient, even when the timeline is uncertain, and even when the wait feels long. Obedience is about trusting that God's timing is perfect and that your preparation will not be in vain.

**The Consequences of Disobedience**

The five foolish virgins also knew their assignment, but their lack of preparation revealed their disobedience. They brought their lamps, but they didn't bring the oil needed to keep them burning. Their failure to anticipate the bridegroom's timing and to prepare adequately meant that when the moment came, they were left scrambling, unready to fulfill their role.

Disobedience in the context of our assignment can be disastrous. The foolish virgins missed the wedding feast because they failed to obey the simple instruction to be ready. Their disobedience cost them a place in the celebration. Similarly, when we fail to obey God's commands and neglect our assignment, we may miss the opportunity to experience the fullness of God's purposes in our lives.

Hebrews 5:9 reminds us that "having been perfected, He became the author of eternal salvation to all who obey Him." The key to unlocking God's eternal purposes in our lives is obedience. As believers, we must align ourselves with God's will, and that alignment can only happen through the anointing of the Holy Spirit.

Disobedience often looks like partial readiness—showing up without being fully equipped, starting without finishing, or accepting the assignment without committing to the preparation it requires. The foolish virgins wanted to be part of the celebration, but they weren't willing to pay the cost of obedience. As a result, they missed the bridegroom's arrival, and the door to the celebration was shut.

**Living in Obedience to God's Assignment**

Beloved, God has called each of us to a unique assignment. That assignment is not always easy, but it is a divine calling that requires both obedience and the empowering presence of the Holy Spirit. The Parable of the Ten Virgins is a powerful reminder that obedience is not just a matter of following orders but a matter of preparation and readiness. Through the anointing of the Holy Spirit, we are enabled to obey, and through obedience, we fulfill our divine assignments.

Living in obedience means more than just showing up—it means being prepared, being faithful, and being willing to bring your best to God's work. Here's what obedience looks like in our daily lives:

1. **Seeking God's Guidance:** Obedience starts with understanding your assignment. Spend time in prayer and study of God's Word to discern His calling for your life.

   ___

   ___

   ___

   ___

2. **Preparing with Intention:** Just as the wise virgins brought extra oil, prepare yourself for the unexpected. Stay connected to God through prayer, worship, and fellowship, so your "oil" is always full.

   ___

   ___

   ___

   ___

3. **Trusting God's Timing:** The bridegroom came at an unexpected hour, but the wise virgins were ready because they trusted that he would come. Trust God's

timing, even when it's not aligned with your expectations.

______________________________________________

______________________________________________

______________________________________________

______________________________________________

4. **Carrying Out the Assignment with Joy:** The bridesmaids' role was to light the bridegroom's way—a role of honor and celebration. Approach your assignment with the same joy and enthusiasm, knowing that your obedience glorifies God.

______________________________________________

______________________________________________

______________________________________________

______________________________________________

**Interactive Element: Reflecting on Your Obedience**

Take some time to reflect on your own life and your obedience to God's calling. Use these prompts to guide your reflection:

- **What is your assignment?** Ask God to reveal the purpose and calling He has placed on your life.

______________________________________________

- **Are you bringing your lamp and your oil?** Consider whether you are fully prepared to fulfill your assignment, or if there are areas where you need to strengthen your readiness.

- **What steps can you take to live more obediently?** Identify specific actions you can take to deepen your relationship with God and to prepare for the work He has called you to do.

Write down your answers and pray for God's guidance as you commit to living in obedience to His will.

## Conclusion: The Power of Obedience

Obedience is the foundation of readiness. It's what enables us to carry out God's assignments with confidence, faith, and effectiveness. The ten virgins were all called to the same assignment, but only the wise virgins fulfilled their role because they were obedient in their preparation.

As you reflect on this chapter, remember that obedience is not just about doing—it's about trusting, preparing, and aligning your heart with God's will. It's about bringing your lamp and your oil, about being ready for whatever God has in store, and about honoring Him with your faithfulness.

Choose today to live a life of obedience. Bring your lamp, keep it filled with oil, and step confidently into the assignments God has prepared for you. The celebration is coming, and when the bridegroom arrives, your readiness will allow you to step fully into the joy and purpose of His calling. Stay obedient, stay ready, and stay filled with His Spirit.

# CHAPTER
SEVEN

## SLIDING into POSITION

### Assignment with Eternal Impact

We are all called to fulfill a divine assignment within our lifetime—something unique, purposeful, and transformative. However, as we walk through life, it's essential to understand that our assignment carries two distinct types of impact: eternal and worldly. These two dimensions are connected, yet different. Both forms of impact are important, but they are different in nature and significance. In order to fulfill our assignment in both the earth and eternally we must remember that they require intentionality, faithfulness, and the anointing of the Holy Spirit to navigate effectively. To illustrate this profound truth, the Parables of the Ten Virgins continues to awaken us to the importance of living out God's assignment and provides an insightful backdrop for understanding the relationship between our assignment, our impact, and the anointing needed to fulfill both.

Not all assignments are created equal. Some are quick and fleeting, while others require endurance, perseverance, and an unwavering commitment to God's call. The Parable of the Ten Virgins reminds us that waiting for the bridegroom wasn't a quick or easy assignment. It required preparation, patience, and a commitment to staying ready for the long haul.

The assignment of the virgins was clear: they were to be ready to meet the bridegroom when he arrived. This was their task, their calling. The virgins had one job—to wait for the bridegroom, prepared with oil.

For us, our assignment is not always as visible as this. Our assignment may seem simple: to live out the calling God has given us, to be faithful in the small things, and to trust His timing. But, like the virgins, it's easy to forget the significance of our assignment, to become distracted or complacent, and to neglect the preparation needed to fulfill it.

The same is true for the assignments God places on our lives. Some tasks may be short and immediate, while others may span months, years, or even a lifetime. The critical question is: are you prepared to sustain the calling? Are you equipped to carry your lamp with enough oil to endure the journey?

## The Prepared and the Unprepared

The ten women in the parable all knew they were on assignment. They all brought their lamps, which represented their commitment to the task. But only five brought the oil needed to keep their lamps burning. All ten were aware of the requirements, but half of them failed to prepare for the reality of waiting. This is where the crisis unfolded.

Beloved, it's a terrible thing to be on assignment and not be prepared. Preparation is more than showing up; it's about ensuring that you have everything you need to carry out the assignment fully. This goes beyond outward readiness—it's about having the inner strength, the spiritual resources, and the anointing to see it through to completion.

## Recognizing the Importance of Oil

The oil in the parable represents the anointing and presence of God in our lives. It's what sustains us, empowers us, and gives us the ability to fulfill our God-given assignments. Without the oil, the lamp is just a decoration—it has no function, no light, and no purpose.

The anointing helps us live intentionally, preparing our hearts and minds for the assignment God has given us. The Holy Spirit equips us with the wisdom to discern when and how to act, and He strengthens us to follow through, even when the waiting is long or the challenges seem overwhelming.

In 1 John 2:27, the Bible says, "But the anointing which you have received from Him abides in you, and you do not need that anyone teach you; but as the same anointing teaches you concerning all things, and is true, and is not a lie, and just as it has taught you, you will abide in Him." The anointing teaches us to abide in Christ and walk in His ways. It enables us to fulfill our divine assignment with purpose and conviction, resulting in eternal impact that will not fade away.

The five foolish virgins had the outward appearance of readiness, but they lacked the oil to sustain their lamps. They were unprepared for the wait, unprepared for the challenges, and ultimately unprepared for the bridegroom's arrival. The five wise virgins, however, understood the importance of the oil. They didn't just bring their lamps; they brought extra oil, knowing that the wait could be long and that they needed to be prepared for anything.

## Preparation Beyond the Surface

Preparation isn't just about finances, education, or resources—although those things are important. True preparation is rooted in your spiritual life. It's about carrying the oil of God's anointing, the power of His presence, and the strength of His Word. Here's why this preparation matters:

1. **The Oil Destroys the Yoke:** Isaiah 10:27 reminds us that it is the anointing of God that destroys the yoke of bondage. The oil is what breaks the chains of fear, doubt, and discouragement that try to hold us back.

   ______________________________________________

   ______________________________________________

   ______________________________________________

   ______________________________________________

2. **The Oil Lights the Way:** Without oil, the lamp cannot shine. The oil is what enables us to be a light in a dark world, to illuminate the path for ourselves and others as we walk in obedience to God.

   ______________________________________________

   ______________________________________________

   ______________________________________________

   ______________________________________________

3. **The Oil Sustains the Assignment:** The journey is often longer than we expect, and challenges will arise. The oil is what sustains us through the waiting, the struggles, and the uncertainties of life.

   ______________________________________________

   ______________________________________________

   ______________________________________________

   ______________________________________________

**Assignment vs. Impact:** An assignment refers to the specific task God gives each believer, a calling to fulfill His purpose in the world. It is a divine mandate—an opportunity to serve, to build, and to carry out God's will on earth. Every believer has a unique assignment, but it is part of the larger body of Christ's mission: to glorify God and bring His Kingdom to earth.

Impact, however, is the result or influence of that assignment. It is the tangible effect of obedience and faithfulness in carrying out the task God has set before us. There are two kinds of impact: eternal and worldly. The eternal impact refers to the lasting change made in the lives of others and the world that aligns with God's purposes and has eternal value. Worldly impact, on the other hand, is the temporary effect we may have on the material world—an influence that is often seen but can fade with time.

Both forms of impact are important, but they are different in nature and significance. The Parable of the Ten Virgins provides an insightful backdrop for understanding the relationship between our assignment, our impact, and the anointing needed to fulfill both.

**Sliding Into Position**

Sliding into position means being ready to move when God calls, prepared to act when the moment arrives, and equipped to sustain the work for as long as it takes. It's about aligning yourself with God's purpose and being ready for His timing, no matter how long the wait.

Here's how you can ensure you're always ready to slide into position:

1. **Fill Your Lamp Daily:** Spend time with God each day, allowing Him to fill you with His presence, His Word, and His strength. Your daily connection with Him is what keeps your oil full.

    ____________________________________________

    ____________________________________________

    ____________________________________________

    ____________________________________________

2. **Anticipate the Wait:** Like the wise virgins, prepare for the unexpected. Assume that the journey will be longer than you think, and make sure you have the spiritual reserves to endure.

   ______________________________________________

   ______________________________________________

   ______________________________________________

   ______________________________________________

3. **Stay Focused on the Assignment:** Don't get distracted by the busyness of life or the opinions of others. Keep your eyes on the bridegroom and the purpose He has called you to fulfill.

   ______________________________________________

   ______________________________________________

   ______________________________________________

   ______________________________________________

4. **Guard Against Complacency:** Complacency is the enemy of readiness. Don't let moments of ease or success lull you into spiritual laziness. Stay vigilant and intentional in your walk with God.

   ______________________________________________

   ______________________________________________

________________________________________

________________________________________

5. **Surround Yourself with the Right People:** The five wise virgins couldn't share their oil, but they set an example of preparation and readiness. Surround yourself with people who inspire you to stay prepared and who challenge you to deepen your relationship with God.

   ________________________________________

   ________________________________________

   ________________________________________

   ________________________________________

**The Dangers of Showing Up Unprepared**

The enemy isn't afraid of your degrees, your titles, or your bank account. What he fears is your oil—your anointing, your connection to God, and your ability to walk in His power. Without oil, you're vulnerable to burnout, discouragement, and defeat. Showing up unprepared doesn't just hinder your ability to fulfill your assignment; it leaves you open to the attacks of the enemy.

In this season, God is calling for laborers who are prepared—not just in the physical sense, but in the spiritual sense. He's looking for people who have taken the time to fill their lamps, who have cultivated their relationship with Him, and who are ready to shine brightly for His glory.

**Interactive Element: Your Preparation Plan**

Take some time to reflect on your readiness to fulfill God's assignment in your life. Use the following prompts to create a plan for staying spiritually prepared:

**Evaluate Your Current Readiness:**

- Do you have the oil you need to sustain your spiritual life?

  ________________________________________

  ________________________________________

  ________________________________________

  ________________________________________

  ________________________________________

- Are there areas where you feel unprepared or lacking?

  ________________________________________

  ________________________________________

  ________________________________________

  ________________________________________

  ________________________________________

  ________________________________________

**Set Specific Goals:**

- How will you fill your lamp daily? (e.g., prayer, Bible study, worship)

_______________________________________________

_______________________________________________

_______________________________________________

_______________________________________________

_______________________________________________

- What steps will you take to deepen your relationship with God?

_______________________________________________

_______________________________________________

_______________________________________________

_______________________________________________

_______________________________________________

**Anticipate Challenges:**

- What obstacles might drain your oil? (e.g., distractions, discouragement, sin)

_______________________________________________

_______________________________________________

_______________________________________________

_______________________________________________

- How will you overcome these challenges and stay focused on your assignment?

______________________________________________

______________________________________________

______________________________________________

______________________________________________

**Create a Weekly Routine:**

- Outline a schedule that prioritizes your spiritual growth. Include time for personal devotion, corporate worship, and fellowship with other believers.

______________________________________________

______________________________________________

______________________________________________

______________________________________________

______________________________________________

______________________________________________

______________________________________________

______________________________________________

______________________________________________

______________________________________________

______________________________________________

______________________________________________

______________________________________________

**Review and Adjust:**

- Regularly assess your progress and make adjustments as needed. Stay flexible and open to God's leading as you navigate your assignment.

  ______________________________________________

  ______________________________________________

  ______________________________________________

  ______________________________________________

**Conclusion: The Difference the Oil Makes**

Beloved, sliding into position requires more than just showing up. It requires intentional preparation, unwavering focus, and a commitment to carrying the oil of God's anointing in your life. The five wise virgins understood this, and their readiness allowed them to fulfill their assignment and enter into the celebration.

As you reflect on this chapter, remember that your oil is what sets you apart. It's what equips you to shine brightly, to endure the journey, and to fulfill the purpose God has placed on your life. Don't wait until the last minute to prepare—start now. Fill your lamp, guard your oil, and stay ready to slide into position when the bridegroom calls.

The wait may be long, but with the oil of God, you'll have everything you need to carry out your assignment with faith, strength, and purpose. Stay prepared, stay focused, and watch as God uses you for His glory.

# CHAPTER
EIGHT

# THE IMPORTANCE of SOBRIETY and WATCHFULNESS

**Expectation, Acceptance, and the Unexpected**

Life has a way of catching us off guard. Blessings and challenges often arrive at unexpected moments, in ways we could never have planned for. The Parable of the Ten Virgins teaches us that unpreparedness doesn't mean a lack of opportunity—it means a missed opportunity. And while unplanned does not mean unwanted or unloved, it does require us to embrace the unexpected with a spirit of acceptance and readiness.

In this chapter, we explore how spiritual sobriety and watchfulness prepare us for the moments when life shifts unexpectedly. The wait may be long, and the night may seem endless, but a cry will come at midnight—a moment of revelation, transition, or opportunity. The question is: will you be ready when the cry goes out?

## Unplanned, But Not Unimportant

Many of us struggle with the idea of the unplanned. We like control, certainty, and predictability. But God's plans often disrupt our routines, calling us to trust Him beyond what we can see or understand. The ten virgins all knew they were waiting for the bridegroom, but they didn't know when he would come. Their waiting wasn't wasted—it was a test of their readiness, patience, and watchfulness.

When something unplanned enters your life, it's easy to fall into frustration or fear. But what if we approached the unplanned with less expectation of how things "should" look and more acceptance of what God is doing in the moment? Being spiritually sober means we are clear-minded, focused on God's purpose, and ready to adjust to His timing, even when it's unexpected.

## The Danger of Drowsiness

The parable says that all ten virgins grew drowsy and fell asleep as the night wore on. Waiting has a way of wearing us down. The longer the wait, the easier it is to lose focus, to become complacent, and to let our guard down. For the foolish virgins, this drowsiness led to disaster—they were not prepared when the bridegroom arrived, and they missed their moment.

**The Devil's Lullaby:** In the Parable of the Ten Virgins, all ten bridesmaids are assigned to the same task—to wait for the bridegroom. However, while the bridegroom delays, all ten virgins grow tired and fall asleep (Matthew 25:5). The wise virgins are eventually prepared, but the foolish ones miss out.

The act of sleeping in this parable is not just physical rest; it symbolizes a spiritual slumber. The devil, knowing how critical it is for us to remain alert and spiritually awake, uses life's challenges, disappointments, and distractions to rock us to sleep. Sometimes, it's not a grand temptation but the mundane struggles and surprises of life that lull us into a sense of comfort or apathy.

These challenges are often unplanned and unexpected. They can be anything from family crises, financial difficulties, health issues, or even the monotony of daily responsibilities. Over time, if we're not careful, we begin to drift into a spiritual slumber, thinking, "It's not so bad," or "I'll wake up when I need to." But the truth is, we may miss the most important moment—our moment of encounter with God or the fulfillment of our assignment.

Sleep is not the issue—it's the state of your heart and spirit when the cry goes out that matters.

**Watchful and Sober:** The Bible tells us to remain watchful and sober in these times of challenge and uncertainty. Being watchful means being alert, aware, and attentive to the voice of the Holy Spirit, discerning the times, and staying spiritually awake. It's easy to get caught up in the routine of life, but we are called to be vigilant, ever mindful that we are in a spiritual battle. The enemy doesn't wait for a convenient time to attack; he seeks to undermine our focus at every turn, to make us spiritually unaware.

1 Peter 5:8 warns, "Be sober, be vigilant; because your adversary the devil walks about like a roaring lion, seeking whom he may devour." This is the soberness the Bible speaks of—being mentally, emotionally, and spiritually prepared for the challenges that come our way. It's a mindset that resists the lure of complacency and stays rooted in the truth of God's Word.

While watchfulness involves keen awareness, soberness is about resisting distractions and staying grounded in God's truth, regardless of the chaos around us.

**The Anointing's Role:** We cannot remain watchful and sober by our own strength. This is where the anointing of the Holy Spirit becomes crucial. The anointing empowers us to discern the spiritual landscape, to stay vigilant when the world is trying to lull us into his traps and snares. It is the Holy Spirit that gives us the strength to be sober-minded, to resist the pull of distractions, and to stay focused on our divine assignment.

The oil provides us with supernatural wisdom, insight, and clarity to navigate through life's unplanned challenges. It helps us remain awake in the midst of distractions and keeps our hearts attuned to God's voice, enabling us to rise above the noise and chaos.

The oil of God also equips us to be spiritually sober, to maintain a disciplined mind and heart. In times of crisis, it helps us maintain clarity and focus, so we don't fall into the trap of reacting impulsively or losing our way. As we rely on the Holy Spirit, we receive the strength to endure and the wisdom to make decisions that align with God's will, even when circumstances seem out of control.

The Parable of the Ten Virgins (Matthew 25:1-13) offers a clear, sobering lesson on the importance of staying awake and alert, especially when we face life's unplanned challenges. As we walk through this passage, we'll explore what it means to be watchful and sober, how the devil tries to lull us into complacency, and how the anointing of the Holy Spirit helps us remain vigilant in times of uncertainty.

**The Dangers of Spiritual Slumber:** If we do not remain watchful and sober, we risk missing the moment of God's visitation. Just as the foolish virgins missed the bridegroom's arrival because they were unprepared, we may miss God's timing for breakthrough, for direction, or for the fulfillment of our calling.

The key difference between the wise and foolish virgins was their level of preparedness. The wise virgins understood that the assignment required more than just the initial enthusiasm—it required endurance, foresight, and vigilance. Their preparation wasn't just for a moment, but for the long haul. They knew they needed to stay awake and ready at all times.

On the other hand, the foolish virgins allowed themselves to be lulled into spiritual slumber. They didn't anticipate the bridegroom's delay, and when the time came, they were unprepared. Life's unplanned challenges had rocked them to sleep, and they weren't ready when the call came.

## The Cry at Midnight

The cry went out at midnight—the time between day and night, joy and sorrow, pain and healing. This is often how God works, showing up at the moment we least expect. Midnight represents transition, the turning point where the old passes away and the new begins. It's a time of revelation, a time when what was hidden becomes visible.

When the cry goes out, it's not just an announcement—it's a call to action. It's a moment of decision, where you must either step into what God has for you or risk missing the opportunity. For the five wise virgins, their preparation allowed them to move immediately. They trimmed their lamps, filled them with oil, and went out to meet the bridegroom. The foolish virgins, on the other hand, realized they were missing what they needed. Their lack of preparation left them scrambling, and ultimately, they were shut out of the celebration.

## The Importance of Sobriety and Watchfulness

Sobriety and watchfulness are about staying spiritually awake, even when the wait is long and the night is dark. They are about being ready for the cry at midnight, prepared to respond to God's call, and equipped to step into His purpose.

1. **Sobriety:** Spiritual sobriety is a clear-minded focus on God's purpose. It means guarding your heart and mind against distractions, staying rooted in His Word, and resisting the temptations that can dull your spiritual

senses.

_______________________________________________

_______________________________________________

_______________________________________________

_______________________________________________

2. **Watchfulness:** Watchfulness is an active awareness of God's timing and leading. It's about staying alert to the movements of His Spirit, discerning the opportunities He places before you, and being ready to act when He calls.

_______________________________________________

_______________________________________________

_______________________________________________

_______________________________________________

**Avoiding Spiritual Complacency**

The danger of spiritual complacency is that it leaves us unprepared for the unexpected. Like the foolish virgins, we can easily become distracted by the passing of time, assuming that God's delay means we have more time to prepare. But the cry at midnight can come at any moment, and we must be ready.

Here are some ways to avoid spiritual complacency:

1. **Stay Rooted in Prayer:** Prayer keeps you connected to God and attuned to His voice. Make daily prayer a priority, even in seasons of waiting.

   ______________________________________________

   ______________________________________________

   ______________________________________________

   ______________________________________________

2. **Meditate on Scripture:** The Word of God is your guide and foundation. Regularly meditate on passages that remind you of the importance of readiness, such as Matthew 25:12-13 and 1 Peter 5:8.

   ______________________________________________

   ______________________________________________

   ______________________________________________

   ______________________________________________

3. **Surround Yourself with Accountability:** Stay connected to a community of believers who will encourage you, challenge you, and hold you accountable in your spiritual walk.

   ______________________________________________

   ______________________________________________

___________________________________________

___________________________________________

4. **Set Spiritual Goals:** Create milestones to measure your growth and keep you focused on staying prepared. For example, commit to memorizing a verse each week or spending an hour in worship each Sunday.

___________________________________________

___________________________________________

___________________________________________

___________________________________________

**The Cry and the Response**

The cry at midnight was a call to action, a moment of transition that revealed the hearts of the ten virgins. For the wise, it was a moment of readiness; for the foolish, it was a moment of regret. When the cry comes in your life—whether it's a call to a new assignment, a moment of testing, or an unexpected blessing—will you be ready?

The Bible teaches us to cry out to God in moments of need, to lift our voices and declare our dependence on Him. When the cry at midnight reveals what is missing, don't hesitate to cry out to God for strength, guidance, and renewal. He is faithful to meet you in your need and to fill you with the oil you require.

**Interactive Element: A Daily Devotional Guide**

To cultivate sobriety and watchfulness, use this daily devotional guide as a tool to stay spiritually ready:

**Morning: Start the Day Watchful**

- **Scripture Reflection:** Read 1 Peter 5:8 and reflect on what it means to be sober and vigilant today.

  ________________________________________

  ________________________________________

  ________________________________________

  ________________________________________

- **Prayer:** Ask God to guard your heart and mind, to keep you focused on His purpose, and to prepare you for the unexpected.

  ________________________________________

  ________________________________________

  ________________________________________

  ________________________________________

## Midday: Check Your Readiness

- **Reflection:** Evaluate your day so far. Are you staying alert, or have distractions crept in?

  ________________________________________

  ________________________________________

  ________________________________________

  ________________________________________

- **Prayer:** Ask God to refocus your heart and to fill you with fresh oil for the rest of the day.

  ________________________________________

  ________________________________________

  ________________________________________

  ________________________________________

## Evening: Prepare for the Cry at Midnight

- **Scripture Reflection:** Read Matthew 25:12-13 and meditate on the importance of being ready.

  ________________________________________

  ________________________________________

  ________________________________________

  ________________________________________

- **Prayer:** Confess any distractions or complacency and ask God to renew your strength and watchfulness.

  ______________________________________________

  ______________________________________________

  ______________________________________________

  ______________________________________________

**Conclusion: Staying Ready for the Cry at Midnight**

The cry at midnight will come—it may be a call to a new season, an unexpected blessing, or the fulfillment of God's promise in your life. Whatever form it takes, your readiness will determine your response. Sobriety and watchfulness are not just about staying awake; they're about staying connected to God, keeping your lamp full of oil, and living each day with a spirit of expectation.

As you move forward, commit to living a life of spiritual sobriety and watchfulness. Be vigilant, be prepared, and trust that God's timing is perfect. When the cry comes, you will be ready to step into your next season with confidence, faith, and the anointing of His Spirit.

______________________________________________

______________________________________________

# CHAPTER
NINE

# STEWARDSHIP of GOD'S GIFTS

**The Responsibility of the Oil**

The parable of the ten virgins offers a profound lesson in stewardship—the wise use and management of the gifts God has entrusted to us. The oil represents more than a resource; it represents the anointing, the presence of God, and the spiritual readiness required to fulfill our assignments. Five women in the parable understood this truth, while the other five ignored it, treating their lamps as sufficient without the sustaining power of extra oil.

Stewardship begins with recognizing the value of what you carry. It's about understanding that your oil—your anointing, your gifts, and your purpose—is unique to you and cannot be borrowed or transferred. God's gifts require intentional care, replenishment, and readiness. You can't rely on someone else's preparation, prayer life, or anointing to sustain you. Beloved, you must *BYOO*—Bring Your Own Oil!

## The Folly of the Unprepared

The five foolish virgins made a critical error: they brought their lamps but failed to bring extra oil. Outwardly, they looked ready. They had their lamps in hand, but when the bridegroom delayed, their lack of preparation was exposed. They underestimated the importance of sustaining their readiness, and when the midnight cry came, they found themselves scrambling to meet the moment.

This is a powerful reminder that we cannot live on appearances alone. It's not enough to look prepared; we must *be* prepared. Stewardship means understanding that the assignments God gives us will require more than surface-level commitment. The foolish virgins treated their lamps as if they were decorations instead of tools. They failed to take ownership of the responsibility God had entrusted to them.

## The Wisdom of the Prepared

In contrast, the five wise virgins exemplified what it means to steward God's gifts. They anticipated the bridegroom's delay and prepared accordingly, bringing extra oil to sustain their lamps. Their actions demonstrate three key principles of stewardship:

1. **Anticipation:** The wise virgins didn't assume the journey would be short or easy. They prepared for the unexpected, understanding that their readiness depended on their ability to sustain the light through the wait.

    ______________________________________________

    ______________________________________________

    ______________________________________________

    ______________________________________________

2. **Ownership:** They recognized that their oil was their responsibility. They didn't rely on others to provide for them or assume that someone else would fill the gap.

    ______________________________________________

    ______________________________________________

    ______________________________________________

    ______________________________________________

3. **Boundaries:** When the foolish virgins asked to borrow their oil, the wise women set boundaries. They understood that sharing their oil would leave them unprepared, compromising their ability to fulfill their assignment. Stewardship includes knowing when to say no.

    ______________________________________________

    ______________________________________________

___________________________________________

___________________________________________

**Why Stewardship Matters**

Stewardship is about managing God's gifts in a way that honors Him and fulfills His purpose. Here's why it's essential:

1. **Your Oil is Unique:** The anointing God has placed on your life is specifically for you. It's tailored to your purpose, your journey, and your calling. Sharing or neglecting your oil diminishes your ability to fulfill your role.

   ___________________________________________

   ___________________________________________

   ___________________________________________

   ___________________________________________

2. **You Don't Know the Timing:** Just as the virgins didn't know when the bridegroom would come, we don't know when God will call us to step into a new season, opportunity, or assignment. Stewardship ensures that we are ready when the time comes.

   ___________________________________________

   ___________________________________________

________________________________________

________________________________________

3. **It's About Endurance:** The journey of faith is often longer and harder than we anticipate. Stewardship equips us to endure the challenges, delays, and difficulties along the way.

________________________________________

________________________________________

________________________________________

________________________________________

**BYOO: Bring Your Own Oil**

The cry at midnight revealed the difference between the wise and the foolish virgins. The wise were able to light their lamps and go to the bridegroom because they had brought their own oil. Meanwhile, the foolish virgins were left scrambling, asking to borrow oil and ultimately missing the opportunity to enter.

Let's make this clear: you cannot rely on someone else's oil to sustain you. You can't live off another person's prayer life, faith, or spiritual preparation. Just as you wouldn't leave home without your wallet or your keys, don't leave home without your oil. It's your responsibility to maintain and steward the anointing God has given you.

### The Practical Side of Stewardship

So how do we steward God's gifts effectively? Here are practical steps to ensure that your oil remains full:

**Daily Refueling:**

- Spend time in prayer and worship every day. This is how you refill your spiritual oil and stay connected to God.

  ____________________________________________

  ____________________________________________

  ____________________________________________

  ____________________________________________

  ____________________________________________

- Meditate on Scripture, allowing God's Word to guide and strengthen you.

  ____________________________________________

  ____________________________________________

  ____________________________________________

  ____________________________________________

  ____________________________________________

1. **Set Boundaries:**

   - Protect your oil by saying no to distractions, toxic relationships, and unnecessary commitments.

     ______________________________________________

     ______________________________________________

     ______________________________________________

     ______________________________________________

   - Be discerning about where you invest your time, energy, and resources.

     ______________________________________________

     ______________________________________________

     ______________________________________________

     ______________________________________________

2. **Anticipate Delays:**

   - Life rarely goes according to plan. Be prepared for challenges, detours, and waiting seasons by staying rooted in faith.

     ______________________________________________

     ______________________________________________

     ______________________________________________

     ______________________________________________

3. **Seek Wisdom:**

    - Surround yourself with wise counsel—people who encourage you, hold you accountable, and help you grow in your faith.

      ______________________________________

      ______________________________________

      ______________________________________

      ______________________________________

4. **Invest in Growth:**

    - Stewardship includes developing your gifts and talents. Take the time to learn, grow, and sharpen your skills for God's glory.

      ______________________________________

      ______________________________________

      ______________________________________

      ______________________________________

**The Consequences of Neglecting Stewardship**

The parable makes it clear: the foolish virgins missed the bridegroom's arrival because they failed to steward their oil. Their lack of preparation not only affected them but also excluded them from the celebration. Neglecting stewardship leads to missed opportunities, unfulfilled potential, and a diminished ability to carry out God's assignments.

On the other hand, the wise virgins entered into the joy of the bridegroom. Their preparation allowed them to fulfill their purpose and experience the fullness of God's blessings. Stewardship is not just about responsibility; it's about stepping into the abundant life God has prepared for you.

**Interactive Element: A Stewardship Plan**

Take a moment to create a plan for stewarding the gifts God has entrusted to you. Use the prompts below to guide your reflection:

**Assess Your Oil:**

- Are there areas in your life where you feel spiritually drained or unprepared?

  ________________________________________

  ________________________________________

  ________________________________________

  ________________________________________

  ________________________________________

- What steps can you take to refill your oil daily?

  ________________________________________

**Identify Your Gifts:**

- What unique talents, skills, or resources has God given you?

- How are you using these gifts to fulfill His purpose?

**Set Boundaries:**

- Are there distractions or relationships that are draining your oil?

______________________________________________

______________________________________________

______________________________________________

- What changes can you make to protect your anointing?

______________________________________________

______________________________________________

______________________________________________

______________________________________________

______________________________________________

**Anticipate Challenges:**

- What potential obstacles might hinder your ability to steward God's gifts?

______________________________________________

______________________________________________

______________________________________________

______________________________________________

______________________________________________

______________________________________________

- How will you prepare to overcome these challenges?

______________________________________________

______________________________________________

______________________________________________

______________________________________

______________________________________

______________________________________

**Conclusion: The Wisdom of a Steward**

A wise woman builds her house, but a foolish woman tears it down. Stewardship is about building—building your faith, your readiness, and your ability to carry out God's assignments. It's about bringing your own oil, guarding what God has entrusted to you, and being ready to step into His purpose at a moment's notice.

As you reflect on this chapter, remember that your oil is precious. It's the key to fulfilling your calling, sustaining your journey, and experiencing the fullness of God's blessings. Commit today to stewarding your gifts with wisdom, diligence, and faithfulness. Never leave home without your oil, because what God has for you is too important to miss. **BYOO—Bring Your Own Oil—and be ready for what God has in store.**

______________________________________

______________________________________

______________________________________

______________________________________

# CHAPTER
TEN

# STAYING READY and REFRESHED

## A Lamp Without Oil Is Just Decoration

In the parable of the ten virgins, readiness is not just about having a lamp; it's about having the oil to keep it burning. The five wise women who brought extra oil teach us a profound lesson about staying prepared and refreshed for what God has in store. They show us that having the oil allows us to see clearly, move swiftly, and live with spiritual sobriety. This chapter will explore how staying ready and refreshed equips us to fulfill our assignments and walk into God's promises with confidence.

## The Oil Allows You to See

The five wise virgins brought extra oil because they understood the importance of being able to see. The oil in their lamps lit their path through the dark night, enabling them to recognize the bridegroom when he arrived. The foolish virgins, on the other hand, were left in darkness, scrambling to find oil when they should have been stepping into their assignment.

## Seeing Requires Light

Without oil, there is no light. Without light, we stumble in darkness, unsure of where we are or where we are going. The oil is what keeps our spiritual vision clear, allowing us to see God's plan, recognize His timing, and avoid unnecessary detours.

## Expecting the Wrong Things

Sometimes we can't see clearly because we are expecting the wrong things. We focus on our own plans instead of aligning ourselves with God's purpose. The foolish virgins assumed the bridegroom would come quickly, but their assumptions left them unprepared for the delay. To see clearly, we must let go of our expectations and trust God's timing.

## Light to Be Seen

Our light is not just for us—it's also for others to see. Jesus calls us the light of the world (Matthew 5:14), and our light shines so that others can glorify our Father in heaven. Keeping your lamp filled with oil ensures that your light is visible, both to guide others and to make you recognizable to the bridegroom.

## Obedience Fuels the Oil

How do we keep our oil replenished? Through obedience. Obedience is better than sacrifice (1 Samuel 15:22), and it is the key to staying ready. When we follow God's instructions, even when they are inconvenient or challenging, we position ourselves to see His plan clearly and to shine brightly.

## The Oil Allows You to Slide In

The wise virgins were ready to slide into position when the bridegroom arrived. Even though they fell asleep during the wait, their preparation ensured they could act immediately when the cry went out. Their readiness gave them access, while the foolish virgins were left scrambling.

## Obedience Grants Access

Sliding into position requires obedience to every step of the assignment, not just the parts we like. Faith unlocks the door, but obedience ensures we have access to walk through it. The wise virgins' obedience in bringing extra oil allowed them to move seamlessly into the celebration.

## Preparation for the Long Haul

Life has a way of lulling us to sleep, but preparation ensures we can respond even in moments of rest. Being prepared in season and out of season (2 Timothy 4:2) means staying ready no matter what life throws at you. The wise virgins were able to slide in before the door shut because they had been in the trenches, prepared for both the good and the bad.

## Faith to Stay the Course

To slide into your position, you must trust God through the entire process. Sometimes we give up too quickly, abandoning our assignments because we grow weary or impatient. The wise virgins teach us to stay the course, trusting that our preparation will pay off when the time comes.

## The Oil Allows You to Be Sober

Sobriety and watchfulness are essential for staying ready. The wise virgins were vigilant, prepared for the bridegroom's arrival even though they didn't know when he would come. They understood that spiritual sobriety requires staying alert, diligent, and intentional.

## Be Watchful

Peter reminds us to *"be sober, be vigilant; because your adversary the devil walks about like a roaring lion, seeking whom he may devour"* (1 Peter 5:8). Sobriety in this context means having a clear mind and an attentive spirit, free from distractions and worldly intoxications.

## Guard Against Oil Leaks

The midnight cry exposed the foolish virgins' lack of preparation. They had allowed their lamps to run dry, leaving them unprepared to meet the bridegroom. Oil leaks in our spiritual lives occur when we neglect prayer, worship, and time in God's Word. Stay watchful so you don't lose what God has given you.

## Diligence in Stewardship

Jesus' parable teaches us to be faithful stewards of the oil God has entrusted to us. This oil can't be wasted or taken for granted. It must be maintained, replenished, and guarded with diligence. Always live in a state of readiness, for you do not know the day or the hour of God's call.

## Stay Ready and Refreshed

Staying ready is not just a command—it's a lifestyle. The five wise virgins understood this, and their preparation allowed them to step into the bridegroom's presence with confidence and joy. The foolish virgins, on the other hand, missed their moment because they failed to steward their oil.

## How to Stay Ready

1. **Keep Your Lamps Full:** Spend time daily in prayer, worship, and God's Word. These practices refill your oil and keep your light shining brightly.

   ______________________________________________

   ______________________________________________

   ______________________________________________

   ______________________________________________

2. **Ask for Refreshing:** When life feels overwhelming, cry out to God for a fresh anointing. His Spirit will breathe new life into you, clearing away the oil crisis and giving you the strength to endure.

   ______________________________________________

   ______________________________________________

______________________________________________

______________________________________________

3. **Live with Expectation:** Always be ready for God's call, trusting that His timing is perfect and His plan is good.

   ______________________________________________

   ______________________________________________

   ______________________________________________

   ______________________________________________

**Prayer of Refreshing:**

"Lord, refresh us. Clear up the oil crisis in our hearts and minds. Do it in Your name, God. Help us to believe again, to trust in what we are expecting. Send Your anointing now, like only You can. Breathe on us with Your Holy Spirit. Give us new oil, more oil, and another level of purity. Let Your power be within us, and give us the victory we need for this season. We need Your oil, Lord. We need Your strength. We need another lamp. Amen."

Beloved, staying ready is not a one-time effort; it's a daily commitment. Keep your lamp filled, your heart expectant, and your spirit refreshed. When the midnight cry comes, you will be prepared to step boldly into God's promises, shining brightly for His glory. **Stay ready, stay refreshed, and let your light shine.**

# About the Author

Pastor Natasha Rouse received her calling to preach the Gospel of the Lord Jesus Christ at the early age of 13. She was licensed to preach God's Word at 16. She was later ordained an itinerant deacon in the African Methodist Episcopal Church at the age of 21 and then an itinerant elder at the age of 23 in the AME Church. Reverend Rouse was the youngest in her class to receive both orders.

Rev. Rouse believes that one of her purposes in life is to teach people about the importance of pursuing purpose and destiny—to become who and what God has called them to be.

When she is not teaching or preaching, Reverend Rouse can be found counseling and edifying wives, young women, engaged and married couples, children and their families, or praying for leaders, friends, families, and the world as a whole.

She has traveled all over the country, teaching and preaching the Gospel of our Lord and Savior, **Jesus Christ**! Her motto is: *"Know Jesus and make Him known everywhere I go."* Her favorite saying is: *"Only what you do for Christ will last!"*

Reverend Rouse is a true and tested gift to the Body of Christ Jesus. She is affectionately called **God's Prophetess**. She has truly been called by God to encourage, equip, enlighten, teach, and preach to a dying world and to those who are lost—the goodness of Jesus Christ.

# Connect with Me

To learn more about Natasha C. Johnson-Rouse or to schedule an appointment, email her at revrouse007@gmail.com.

**Social Media:**

Facebook: Natasha Johnson Rouse
Instagram: revladyrouse

www.ingramcontent.com/pod-product-compliance
Lightning Source LLC
Chambersburg PA
CBHW040540170726
48295CB00012B/542

* 9 7 8 1 9 5 5 1 0 7 0 9 9 *